THE STORY OF
PYGMALION

THE STORY OF
PYGMALION

Pamela Espeland

pictures by Catherine Cleary

Carolrhoda Books, Inc., Minneapolis

LIBRARY OF CONGRESS CATALOGING IN PUBLICATION DATA

Espeland, Pamela, 1951-
   The story of Pygmalion.

   SUMMARY: Pygmalion, a sculptor, falls in love with
one of his statues and intercedes with Venus to help.

   1. Pygmalion—Juvenile literature. 2. Galatea—Juvenile literature. [1. Pygmalion. 2. Galatea. 3. Mythology,
Roman] I. Cleary, Catherine. II. Title.

PZ8.1.E83sw   1980   292'.13 [E]   80-15792
ISBN 0-87614-127-0 (lib. bdg.)   AACR1
   2   3   4   5   6   7   8   9   10   92   91   90   89   88   87   86   85   84   83   82

to David Porter, who loves what he teaches
—P.E.

to my supportive husband, Todd
—C.C.

ABOUT THIS STORY

Ancient Greece wasn't very big, but it was very important. All together, the Greek states made up an area about the size of Austria. From this tiny part of the world came many famous people and ideas.

The ancient Greek people were a lot like us. Over 2,000 years ago, their children played and went to school and watched the Olympic games. Grown-ups worked. They wrote plays and poems. They made laws. Their government was the beginning of Western democracy.

But the Greeks didn't know as much as we do about science. So they used myths to explain nature. When there was a storm at sea, they said, "Poseidon, the God of the Sea, must be angry!" When there was a good harvest, they said, "Demeter, the Goddess of the Earth, must be happy!" Not all myths explained nature, though. Some told about Greek history. And some were just good stories.

The Greek civilization lasted for a long time, but it could not last forever. Around 150 B.C., the Romans took it over. They also adopted the Greek gods and goddesses—they just changed their names to Roman names. (In this story the Roman names have been used.) Most Romans didn't really believe in the gods, but they did like to tell good stories. So they kept on telling the myths.

ITALY

BLACK SEA

MT. OLYMPUS

GREECE

PAPHOS

CYPRUS

MEDITERRANEAN SEA

AFRICA

Pygmalion lived on the island of Cyprus.

The story of Pygmalion was first written by a Roman poet named Ovid. Ovid's most famous book is called *Metamorphoses*. The word "metamorphoses" means changes. Each of the poems in the book tells a story about some kind of change. In this story both Pygmalion and his statue change.

Many people have enjoyed the story of Pygmalion. Artists have painted pictures about it. An English writer named George Bernard Shaw wrote a play about it. You may even have seen the movie that was made out of the play. The movie was called *My Fair Lady.*

Long ago, on an island called Cyprus in the Mediterranean Sea, there lived a man named Pygmalion. Pygmalion was a sculptor. He made beautiful statues out of stone and ivory. Sometimes he made statues of heroes. Sometimes he made statues of gods and goddesses. Sometimes he made statues of little children. Pygmalion's statues were wonderful. They looked like real people. Some people thought they looked better than real people.

Pygmalion was a very handsome man. Many young women on Cyprus liked him. But he ignored them all. He didn't like women.

"Women are too much trouble," he said.

Pygmalion was sure he would never get married.
"I am an artist," he said. "I don't need a wife to
bother me. I love my art. That is enough for me."

One day Pygmalion decided to begin a new statue. He chose a block of gleaming marble. Then he picked up his hammer and chisel. He began to work. All day long he worked. And when the sun went down, he lit a fire and kept on working.

Pygmalion had a special feeling about this statue. It almost seemed as if it were trying to jump right out of the stone. He had carved a lot of statues, but never one like this. This statue was different somehow.

Pygmalion worked on his statue for many days. It was a statue of a young woman. It had a gentle, wise face. It had round, smooth shoulders. It was slim and graceful. In the flickering light of the fire, it seemed to breathe.

Sometimes Pygmalion put down his tools and just stared at his statue. He reached out to touch it. How nice it felt! Pygmalion thought it was more beautiful than any real woman he had ever seen.

Before he knew what was happening, Pygmalion fell in love with his statue. He hugged it. He kissed it. And he wanted it to hug and kiss him back. But of course it didn't. It just stood there. After all, it was only a statue.

Poor Pygmalion! He tried hard to forget that the statue was not a real woman. He dressed it like a queen in beautiful robes of purple and gold. He bought it presents —pet birds in silver cages, clever little toys, pieces of

amber. He put diamond rings on its fingers. He wrapped
pearls around its neck. He hung ruby earrings from its
ears. At night he tucked the statue into bed. He covered
it with furs. He even put a feather pillow under its head.

Pygmalion's tools lay in a corner getting dusty. He had stopped making other statues. Instead he spent all his time with the statue he loved. He talked to it for hours. He told it stories.

Sometimes he got angry with himself. "How can I be so stupid?" he would say. "How can I be in love with a piece of stone?" But then he would look at his beautiful statue and fall in love all over again.

Pygmalion thought his love was a secret. He was sure no one else knew about it. But the gods and goddesses always knew what people were up to. One day Venus, the Goddess of Love, looked down from her home on Mount Olympus. She saw how much Pygmalion loved his statue.

"Well, well!" she said, smiling to herself. "Look what has happened to Pygmalion! He said he would never love a woman, and this is what he gets. He falls madly in love with a piece of cold stone! It serves him right!"

But soon Venus started to feel sorry for Pygmalion. After all, she was the Goddess of Love. She wanted people to fall in love with each other. But this was different. Pygmalion wasn't in love with a person. He was in love with a statue. And that would never work!

All of the people on Cyprus worshiped Venus. She was their favorite goddess. Every year they held a special festival for her. People came from all over Cyprus to worship her. They covered her altars with roses, her favorite flower. They brought her white cows whose

horns were wrapped in gold. They prayed to her all day.
They sang songs to her all night.

Pygmalion could hardly stand to leave his statue for
even a minute. But he wanted to worship Venus. He also
wanted to ask her a favor. So he went to one of her altars.

Venus made herself invisible so Pygmalion would not see her. She watched as he laid a gift on her altar and knelt to pray.

"Please listen to me, dear Venus!" he said. "You know that I never liked women. You know that I said I would never get married. But I've changed! I really have! Now I *want* to get married! If only—"

Suddenly he stopped. How could he say, "If only I could marry my statue?" That would sound silly. Even Venus would think so!

Pygmalion thought hard for a few minutes. Then he cleared his throat. He said, "If only I could find someone *just like* my statue! I know I would love her! And I would marry her. I promise!"

Pygmalion's prayer made Venus very happy. So she made the fire on her altar jump up three times. Pygmalion watched the flames get brighter. "I wonder what this means?" he said. "Did Venus hear me? Will she give me what I want?"

Pygmalion hurried home. He could hardly wait to get there. Maybe, just maybe, Venus would answer his prayer.

Pygmalion ran into his house. He looked eagerly around the room. There was his statue waiting for him. Only that morning he had dressed it in a long robe and wrapped gold chains around its neck. He had even put flowers in its hair. It looked beautiful to him. But it was still only a statue. It was only cold stone. Nothing Pygmalion did could ever change that.

Pygmalion felt very sad. He walked slowly over to his statue. He touched its smooth cheek. He saw the rings on its fingers and the tiny slippers he had put on its feet. He put his arms around it. He thought his heart would break.

"It's hopeless!" he cried. "I should have known better than to ask Venus for such an impossible favor!"

But wait! Something strange was happening! Was the statue breathing? Was it moving just a little bit? Was it trying to put its arms around him too?

Pygmalion stepped back. The statue seemed to look right at him. And then it blinked! Pygmalion could hardly

believe his eyes. His statue had become a real woman!
She walked toward him, smiling. He felt her soft breath
on his cheek. Her hair was like silk, and she smelled
like a million flowers. Pygmalion had never been happier.
Venus had answered his prayer!

Of course Pygmalion kept his promise to Venus. He married the woman—her name was Galatea—and Venus came to their wedding. A year later they had a daughter. They called her Paphos. And there is a town in Cyprus named after Paphos that is still there today.

PRONUNCIATION GUIDE

Cyprus: SIE-pruss
Demeter: de-MEE-ter
Galatea: gal-uh-TEE-uh
Metamorphoses: met-uh-MORE-fuh-seez
Olympus: oh-LIM-puss
Ovid: OV-id
Paphos: PAY-foss
Poseidon: poe-SIE-dun
Pygmalion: pig-MAIL-yun
Venus: VEE-nuss